# I'm a Christian Now!

## Younger Kids Activity Book

Beth Bowman                Stephanie Livengood
Kelli McAnally             Kristen White

LifeWay Press®
Nashville, TN 37234

ISBN 978-1-535914-07-9
Item 005805596

DEWEY: J248.82
SUBHD: CHILDREN--RELIGIOUS LIFE \ DISCIPLESHIP \ REGENERATION (CHRISTIANITY)

Printed in the United States of America

Kids Ministry Publishing
LifeWay Church Resources
One LifeWay Plaza
Nashville, Tennessee 37234-0172

We believe the Bible has God for its author; salvation for its end;
and truth, without any mixture of error, for its matter
and that all Scripture is totally true and trustworthy.
To review LifeWay's doctrinal guideline,
please visit www.lifeway.com/doctrinalguideline.

# YOU ARE A CHRISTIAN NOW!

## PARENTS,

What an exciting time in your life and the life of your child. There is nothing more important than your child trusting in Jesus and having a relationship with Him. There is also no greater joy for you as a parent than the privilege of discipling your child in his faith.

This book will guide you as you teach your family the next steps of what it means to be a follower of Jesus and how to live for Him. Use this book each week. Set aside time to complete the family devotions together. Then, encourage your child as she completes each daily devotional page with you or on her own. These devotions reinforce the family devotions you lead.

Through this resource, you will help your child grow in his faith and learn more about God, Jesus, the Bible, the church, and more. This book will help you get started.

## HOW TO USE THIS BOOK

- Read each weekly devotional with your child.
- Review daily devotionals. Encourage your child not to skip a day or do more than one day at a time, but to take the time he needs to understand the information.
- Find a quiet place to study together.
- Pray, asking God to help you learn what He wants you to know as you lead your family.

## THINGS TO HAVE WHEN YOU USE THIS BOOK

- Bible
- Pen or pencil

## THE ABCs

If your child needs help telling someone about Jesus, remember to review the ABCs.
- A-Admit to God that you are a sinner.
- B-Believe that Jesus is God's only Son.
- C-Confess your faith in Jesus as your Savior and Lord.

## CHRISTIAN [KRISS chuhn]

is the name given to a person who has asked Jesus to be his Savior and Lord.

## For Parents:
# LEADING KIDS IN USING THIS BOOK

### MEETING 1: BECOMING A CHRISTIAN

Your child will learn about the most important truth in the world: the gospel. The gospel is the good news of God's plan to redeem us from sin through Jesus' life, death, and resurrection. While the gospel is the specific focus of week one, it's also the foundational truth of Christianity that a believer never moves past. As such, you'll want to continue to revisit the following gospel outline and Scripture passages with your child. Use page 64 to help you.

•Day One: God Rules (Read Revelation 4:11.)
•Day Two: We Sinned (Read Romans 3:23.)
•Day Three: God Provided (Read John 3:16.)
•Day Four: Jesus Gave (Read Romans 5:8.)
•Day Five: We Respond (Read 1 John 1:9.)

### MEETING 2: KNOWING I'M A CHRISTIAN

Your child will begin to examine the relationship between the gospel and the evidence it produces in a Christian's life. Be aware that in learning about healthy Christian habits (prayer, Bible reading, witnessing, etc.), kids may be tempted to think these habits are what save them.

As you lead your child through his activity pages, take time each day to explain that the steps we take to obey God are not what save us. Explain to your child that these steps are a response of joyful obedience to the gospel. We obey God's Word because we love Him. Review the framework of the gospel from week one and see if your child can describe the gospel in his own words by the end of the week.

### MEETING 3: FOLLOWING JESUS' EXAMPLE

Your child will learn about the two ordinances of Christianity: baptism and the Lord's Supper. She will likely have a lot of questions. This is a good thing! Explain to your child what baptism and the Lord's Supper look like as they're practiced at your church. Let your child attend a church service with you where she can observe these acts of worship.

Remind your child that baptism and the Lord's Supper are symbols of the gospel. Read Romans 6:3-4 and Matthew 26:26-28 together. Discuss with her what these symbols represent and how they remind us of Jesus.

### MEETING 4: I'M PART OF A CHURCH

Your child will learn what it means to be part of a church. Kids typically think of the church as a building. Reinforce the truth that the local church is not a building but a group of baptized believers.

Read 1 Corinthians 12:12-27 with your child, which describes the church as a body with many parts. Talk about the ways God has designed the different parts of your child's body to work together. Then draw connections to the ways God has designed different people in your local church to work together. Teach your child that while there are many differences among members of your local church, everyone shares one thing in common—faith in Jesus Christ as Savior!

## MEETING 5: LIVING AS A CHRISTIAN

Your child will learn about the importance of maintaining healthy spiritual disciplines. Ask your child to name some ways he takes care of his body (eating well, exercising, brushing teeth, sleep, and so forth). Draw a connection between how these activities affect physical health and how godly disciplines affect a person's spiritual health.

As you lead your child through his activity book, be honest about your experiences with spiritual disciplines, such as prayer, Bible study, giving, and worship. Share your successes and struggles. Consider ways you can engage together this week. For example, study a chapter of the Bible and journal together or let your child help you write your tithe check or online gift to your church.

## MEETING 6: SHARING YOUR TESTIMONY

Your child will practice sharing the gospel with others. Help in this by sharing your story of coming to faith in Christ. Who shared the gospel with you? What was going on in your life at the time? How did your life change after becoming a Christian? As your child hears you express your testimony of God's salvation, she will grow comfortable doing the same.

Read Acts 1:1-20 with your child. Focus on verse 20, which talks about not being able to stay quiet about the gospel. Ask your child who she thinks needs to hear the gospel. Begin praying for these people every night. Ask God for opportunities to speak to others about Jesus.

## MEETING 7: GOING ON MISSION

Your child will learn about the importance of living on mission for God. Help frame the activity pages by explaining there are two kinds of missions your child can be involved in: 1) missions happening in your zip code and 2) missions happening in faraway places.

Talk about ways your church is involved in both kinds of missions. If your church supports missionaries, spend time praying for them with your child. Read Romans 10:14 together. Discuss that while mission activities may look different from one location to the next, all mission work is to help people hear and believe the good news of Jesus' gospel.

## MEETING 8: TRAVELING ON

Your child will learn about grace (receiving a blessing one doesn't deserve) and mercy (not receiving punishment one does deserve). She will also learn Christians are not perfect. Instead, believers trust in a perfect Savior who offers forgiveness to those who repent.

As you lead your child through the activity pages, tie these concepts to the gospel. Point out that Jesus provided mercy by taking on punishment for sinners and that He provides grace by offering forgiveness and God's favor. Ask your child how many people in the world are perfect. Remind her there is only one perfect person, Jesus, and that He gives His perfect righteousness to Christians. Ask her what other questions she has about following Jesus as a new Christian.

# WEEK 1

# BECOMING A CHRISTIAN

**Parents:** Your child will learn about the most important truth in the world: the gospel. While the gospel is the specific focus of week one, it's also the foundational truth of Christianity that a believer never moves past. As such, you'll want to continue to revisit the following gospel outline and Scripture passages with your child. Use page 64 to help you.

Think about the last few days. What are some decisions you have had to make? Did you decide
• which shoes you should wear?
• whether or not to do your homework?
• what you wanted to eat for an afternoon snack?

When you became a Christian, you made the most important decision of your life. In the next few weeks you will be learning the meaning of some words Christians use, and you will be able to understand what it means to believe in Jesus as your Savior.

Do you know these **ABCs**?
**ADMIT:** Admit to God you are a sinner.
**BELIEVE:** Believe that Jesus is God's one and only Son
**CONFESS:** Confess your faith in Jesus as your Savior and Lord.

**LEARN IT**

CHRISTIAN [KRISS chuhn] The name given to people who have confessed Jesus as their Savior and Lord

JESUS - God's one and only Son

ADMIT - own up to or agree

BELIEVE - to know and trust that something is true

CONFESS - to tell

**KNOW IT**

Jesus provided the way for you to become a Christian. With an adult's help, find John 3:16 in your Bible. Does this sound familiar to you? It is your memory verse for the week!

Find John 3:16 in your Bible. Memorize this verse with your family this week. Circle the correct words to complete your memory verse!

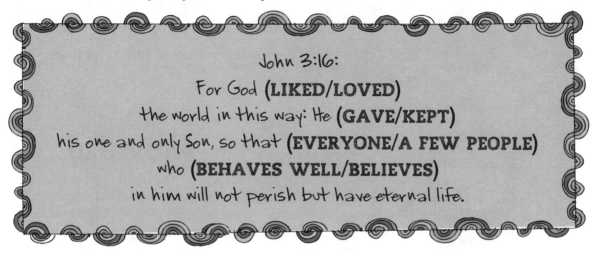

John 3:16:
For God (LIKED/LOVED)
the world in this way: He (GAVE/KEPT)
his one and only Son, so that (EVERYONE/A FEW PEOPLE)
who (BEHAVES WELL/BELIEVES)
in him will not perish but have eternal life.

**DO IT**

The Gospel: God's Plan for Me: Fill in the blanks with the correct word from the word bank, and then number the statements in the order they should go. Check the picture on page 64 if you need help!

_____ SINNED

GOD _____

_____ GIVES

_____ PROVIDED

WE _____

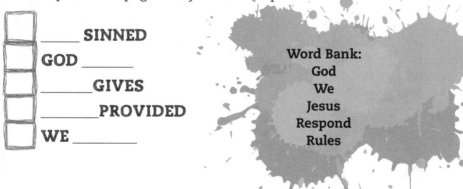

Word Bank:
God
We
Jesus
Respond
Rules

**PRAY IT**

Thank God for loving you and for sending Jesus. Thank Him for helping you know how to become a Christian.

_____

_____

_____

_____

WEEK 1 ✳ DAY 1

# BECOMING A CHRISTIAN

LEARN IT

## DRAW LINES

from the symbol to its two-word meaning.  See page 64 if you need help.

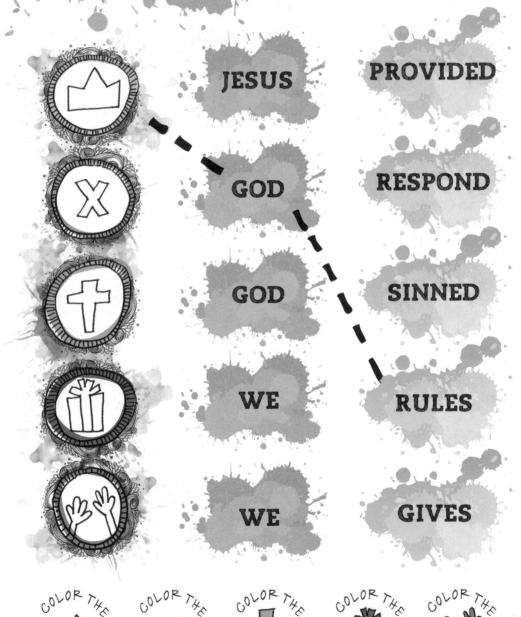

JESUS     PROVIDED

GOD     RESPOND

GOD     SINNED

WE     RULES

WE     GIVES

COLOR THE   YELLOW   God Rules.

COLOR THE   ORANGE   We Sinned.

COLOR THE   BLUE   God Provided.

COLOR THE   RED   Jesus Gives.

COLOR THE   GREEN   We Respond.

**PRAY IT**

## ABCs OF PRAYER

Fill in the missing letters to complete the words in red below. Copy the letters in order to solve the puzzle and discover the new word. When you are done with the puzzle, read the page aloud.

When you pray to become a ☐☐☐☐☐☐☐☐☐ you:

### ADMIT THAT YOU ARE A SINNER.

Tell God you messed up and you are sorry for doing your own thing and turning away from Him through your thoughts, words, and

A☐TIONS. Repent and turn away from your sin.

### BELIEVE THAT JESUS IS GOD'S SON AND ACCEPT GOD'S GIFT OF FORGIVENESS.

Tell God that you believe T☐AT only Jesus can save you and you

cannot save YOU☐SELF from your S☐N problem.

### CONFESS YOUR FAITH IN JESUS CHRIST AS SAVIOR AND LORD.

Tell God and tell OTHER☐ that Jesus is your Lord and

☐HAT He is ☐N charge and C☐LLING the shots in your

life. You are GIVE☐ eternal life and

look forward to being with God forever.

# BECOMING A CHRISTIAN

## DO IT

## CROSS OUT

all of **X, Y,** and **Z** letters below.
Fill in the remaining letters
to solve the puzzle.

_ _ _ _ is my _ _ _ _ _ and _ _ _ _ _ _ .

START

### LORD
Another name for God that means "God is the owner of the earth." It can mean "Master" or "one to whom all things belong." Read Genesis 12:1-4 and Psalm 114:7.

### SAVIOR
One who saves others. Jesus is the Savior. By dying on the cross, Jesus took the penalty for sin and offers salvation. Read John 4:39-42 and 2 Timothy 1:10.

# BECOMING A CHRISTIAN

**FIND IT** **FIND** all the letters and numbers in each color, and write them in the correct box below.

V B O 3
I E A L
E 1
N G O E H
V G O D V D
E 6 L J E

**ARRANGE**
THE RED
LETTERS
INTO THE
MEMORY VERSE
REFERENCE.

**ARRANGE**
THE BLUE
LETTERS
INTO ONE WORD
TO DISCOVER
WHO PROVIDED
FOR US.

**ARRANGE**
THE GREEN
LETTERS
INTO ONE WORD
TO DISCOVER
WHAT HE DID
FOR US.

**ARRANGE**
THE ORANGE
LETTERS
INTO A SECOND
WORD TO
DISCOVER WHAT
HE DID FOR US.

**ARRANGE**
THE YELLOW
LETTERS
INTO ONE WORD
TO DISCOVER
WHAT YOU
CAN DO.

# BECOMING A CHRISTIAN

**LIVE IT**

**USE THE PICTURES** to correctly fill in the words in the sentences below. Read the statements with the motions indicated.

I CAN _admit_ THAT I HAVE _____.

I CAN _____ THAT _____ IS _____.

I CAN _____ MY _____ IN _____.

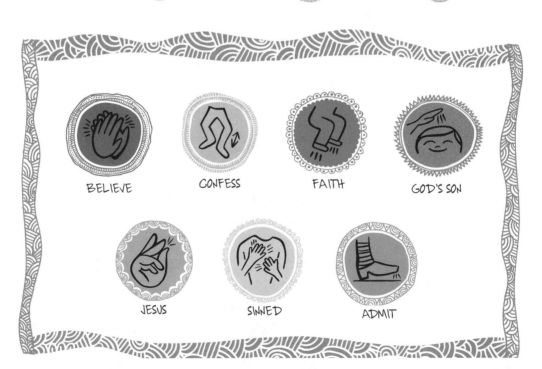

BELIEVE    CONFESS    FAITH    GOD'S SON

JESUS    SINNED    ADMIT

# WEEK 2

# KNOWING I'M A CHRISTIAN

PARENTS

This week guide your child to examine the relationship between the gospel and the evidence it produces in a Christian's life. As you lead your child through his activity pages, take time each day to explain that the steps we take to obey God are not what saves us. These steps are a response of joyful obedience to the gospel. We obey God's Word because we love Him. Review the framework of the gospel from week one and see if your child can describe the gospel in his own words by the end of the week.

Do you know anyone who has been saved from danger? Firemen, doctors, nurses, emergency medical teams, and rescue workers help save lives every day. The word "save" is used in many different ways. When you became a Christian, you probably heard that Jesus saved you from your sin. Jesus is the Savior.

What do you think saved means? Print a short answer here. _____
_____

Do you know why Jesus saves you? Is it because of something good that you did? No! Jesus saves you because He loves you and wants you to be part of His family. When you become a Christian, God changes you. His love does not depend on what we do or how we act, but on what Jesus has already done for us by taking our sin on the cross and giving us new life.

Christians obey God by doing things like praying and reading the Bible, but these activities are a response to being saved — not what saves you! We all sin, so nothing that we do can be good enough to save ourselves. We need Jesus to be the perfect Savior.

**LEARN IT**    SIN – actions, attitudes, words, or thoughts that do not please God

REPENT [ree Pent] to turn from disobeying God to obeying Him

SAVIOR – Jesus, the Person who paid the penalty for your sin

**KNOW IT**

Read Matthew 1:21 in your Bible. Memorize this verse with your family this week. Finish the words below to find out what Jesus did about sin. The first letter of each word is already given.

S ☐ ☐ ☐    U ☐    F ☐ ☐ ☐

O ☐ ☐    S ☐ ☐

**DO IT**

In the clouds below, print things that you think are sins.

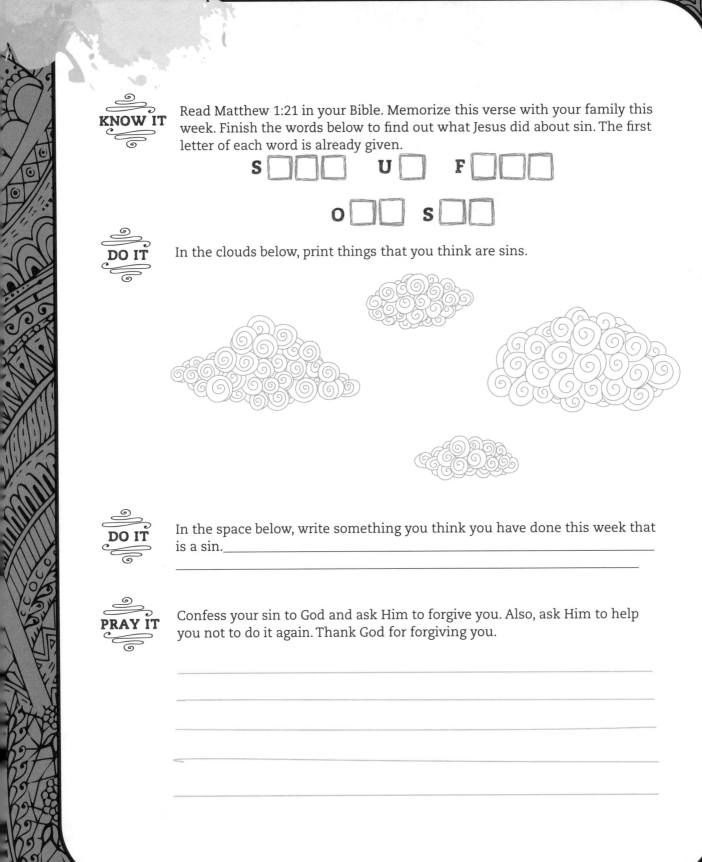

**DO IT**

In the space below, write something you think you have done this week that is a sin. _____

_____

**PRAY IT**

Confess your sin to God and ask Him to forgive you. Also, ask Him to help you not to do it again. Thank God for forgiving you.

_____

_____

_____

_____

# KNOWING THAT I'M A CHRISTIAN

 **LEARN IT** **FILL IN** each blank with the correct letter, using the answer key:

A E I O U

J □S□S
God's one and only Son

HOLY SP□R□T
Helps people understand and accept God's plan of salvation

S△V□□R
One who saves others

ADM□T
To own up to or to agree

R□P□NT
To turn or change from disobeying God to obeying Him

S□NS
Actions, attitudes, words, or thoughts that do not please God

B□L□□V□
To know and trust that something is true

C□NF□SS
To tell

B△PT□SM
When someone who is already a Christian is lowered into the water and brought back up as a way to show others that he has confessed Jesus as Savior and Lord

CHR□ST□△N
Name given to people who have confessed Jesus as their Savior and Lord

## DO YOU KNOW THESE ABCs?

ADMIT: Admit to God you are a sinner.

BELIEVE: Believe that Jesus is God's One and Only Son.

CONFESS: Confess your faith in Jesus as your Savior and Lord.

# KNOWING THAT I'M A CHRISTIAN

 **PRAY IT** 1 Thessalonians 5:17 says to pray constantly.

## WHERE CAN YOU PRAY?

H+ 🐭 -M= _ _ _ _ _

SCH+ 🛁 -P= _ _ _ _ _

CHU+ (letter grid) -WORDSEA= _ _ _ _ _

P+ 🐕 ↑ -B= _ _ _ _ _

## WHEN CAN YOU PRAY?

Write one of the words (sad, frustrated, happy, crying) on the line under the face it matches.

I CAN PRAY WHEN I'M    I CAN PRAY WHEN I'M    I CAN PRAY WHEN I'M    I CAN PRAY WHEN I'M

_ _ _ _ _    _ _ _ _ _    _ _ _ _ _    _ _ _ _ _

# KNOWING THAT I'M A CHRISTIAN

**DO IT**

## MYSTERY PICTURE COLOR KEY

**Y** = YELLOW **B** = BLUE

| | |
|---|---|
| 1 | 3Y, 1B, 3Y |
| 2 | 3Y, 1B, 3Y |
| 3 | 1Y, 5B, 1Y |
| 4 | 3Y, 1B, 3Y |
| 5 | 3Y, 1B, 3Y |
| 6 | 3Y, 1B, 3Y |
| 7 | 3Y, 1B, 3Y |

HINT: Follow the color key to color each square in the rows across.
First row: 3 yellow squares, 1 blue square, 3 yellow squares

1
2
3
4
5
6
7

Say your memory verse (Matthew 1:21) aloud to someone. Then make a card to give someone. Include your memory verse. Inside the card, tell that person why Jesus is important to you.

What does this picture help you remember about Jesus? Read Matthew 1:21 for a hint.

17

# KNOWING THAT I'M A CHRISTIAN

## FIND IT

**FIND** I John 1:9 in your Bible. Say this verse to a parent. Cross out each word from this verse to reveal a secret message.

SINS UNRIGHTEOUSNESS I AND IF

OUR ALL

FAITHFUL WE

US KNOW

OUR CLEANSE RIGHTEOUS FORGIVE

TO SINS CONFESS FROM

US US AND IS HE

TO AND

Write the two words that are left in the blanks:

 _____ CAN _____
THAT I'M A CHRISTIAN!

18

# KNOWING THAT I'M A CHRISTIAN

**LIVE IT**

**DRAW** the pictures (or use the colors) in the empty boxes so that no row, column, or group of any four squares has the same picture (or color).

HINT: Which picture (or color) is missing from this row?

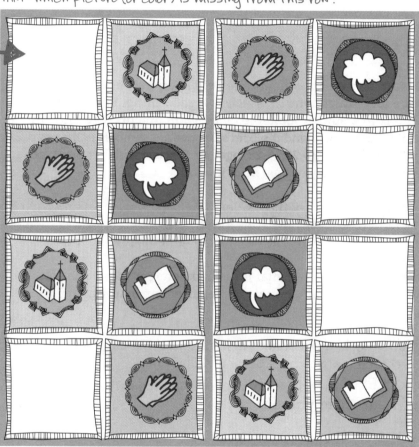

Now that I'm a Christian, I will

READ MY BIBLE

GO TO CHURCH

PRAY TO GOD

TELL MY FRIENDS ABOUT JESUS

Read the following questions and talk through your answers with a parent.

- When did you first start thinking about becoming a Christian?

- Why did you think you needed to become a Christian?

- Explain what happened when you became a Christian.

- How is your life different since you became a Christian?

- How would you help someone know how to become a Christian?

Thank God for sending Jesus to save you. Ask God to help you tell others.

# WEEK 3

# FOLLOWING JESUS' EXAMPLE

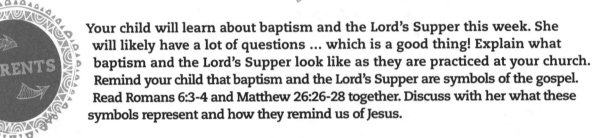

**PARENTS**

Your child will learn about baptism and the Lord's Supper this week. She will likely have a lot of questions … which is a good thing! Explain what baptism and the Lord's Supper look like as they are practiced at your church. Remind your child that baptism and the Lord's Supper are symbols of the gospel. Read Romans 6:3-4 and Matthew 26:26-28 together. Discuss with her what these symbols represent and how they remind us of Jesus.

Have you ever played the game Follow the Leader? One person chooses an activity, and everyone else has to copy him! If he waves his arms, the rest of the group waves their arms too. The leader sets an example, and everyone else has to remember to do it too!

The first church members wanted to remember what Jesus had done for them. They followed two of Jesus' examples to remember His death, burial, and resurrection: baptism and the Lord's Supper.

**LEARN IT**

BAPTISM – a public declaration of faith in Jesus and being put under water to tell others in the church that you have become a Christian

THE LORD'S SUPPER – a special time where the church gathers together to remember Jesus' death and resurrection

**KNOW IT**

Find 1 John 2:6 in your Bible and read it aloud.
How does this verse say you should walk if you follow Jesus? _____

Baptism and the Lord's Supper are two of Jesus' commands for Christians. When you follow these commands, you are walking like Him! Memorize this verse with your family this week.

BAPTISM: "I baptize you in the name of the Father, the Son, and the Holy Spirit," Pastor David said as he put Anita under the water. As Anita came out of the water, she wiped the water from her eyes and smiled. Pastor David helped her to the steps. Everyone in the church was excited for her! What just took place in Anita's life? She was baptized. By being baptized she was showing her church and family that she had become a Christian.

Jesus commanded His believers to be baptized. When you are baptized, you are obeying Jesus. Being baptized shows people that you have become a Christian.

**DO IT**  Baptism is a picture of Jesus' death, burial, and resurrection. Different churches have different places for baptism. Draw a picture of the way your church does baptism.

Have you ever been to the place where your church baptizes? If not, ask your parents or another adult to take you to visit the baptismal area. If it is a baptistry and there is no water in it, walk down into the area and see what it feels like. Talk with your parents or another adult about what it means to be baptized.

## THE LORD'S SUPPER:
Have you ever been on a trip away from home? Was it a family vacation? Maybe you went to the beach or the lake, a family member's house, or a place you had never been before! Did you bring anything back with you to remember your trip? Sometimes people buy souvenirs or take pictures so they can remember important things they saw.

Jesus gave His disciples another way to remember Him. On the night before Jesus died on a cross, He ate dinner with His disciples. During the dinner, Jesus took bread and showed it to the men. He told them the bread was like His body that would be broken. Jesus also took a cup and showed it to the disciples. He said the juice in the cup was like His blood, and it would be poured out for them.

Your church still remembers the special meal Jesus had with His disciples by sharing a similar meal with each other. This special supper is different from other meals. Only two things are served at this meal. Churches do not have this meal because people are hungry. Churches have this meal to remember Jesus' death and resurrection. This meal is called the Lord's Supper.

**DO IT**  Read Luke 22:17-19 in your Bible. The way in which you take part in the Lord's Supper is important. Circle things you can do during the Lord's Supper. Cross out the things you should not do.

Remember why Jesus chose to die and how much He loves you
Confess your sins and ask God to forgive you
Play video games or watch silly videos
Whisper to the people around you
Thank God for Jesus
Be quiet so you and the people around you can think about Jesus and pray to God
Run around the church with your friends
Daydream or fall asleep in your seat

**PRAY IT**  Thank God that baptism and the Lord's Supper can help you remember important things about Jesus. Ask God to help you know the right time for you to be baptized.

# FOLLOWING JESUS' EXAMPLE

## LEARN IT

**WRITE** the first letter of each picture in the blanks to find two important symbols for every Christian.

**THE FIRST CHURCH MEMBERS** followed two of Jesus' examples to remember His death, burial, and resurrection: baptism and the Lord's Supper.

**BAPTISM:** a public declaration of faith in Jesus and being put under water to tell others in the church that you have become a Christian

**LORD'S SUPPER:** a special time where the church gathers together to remember Jesus' death and resurrection

## FIND IT

**GET PERMISSION** from a parent to write in your Bible, and then grab a highlighter and mark any important words from the two stories we studied this week: Jesus' baptism in Matthew 3:13-17 and the first Lord's Supper in 1 Corinthians 11:23-26.

### WORD BANK
for Matthew 3:13-17

baptized
fulfill
Spirit of God
voice from heaven
take delight

### WORD BANK
for 1 Corinthians 11:23-26

bread
body
remembrance
cup
new covenant
drink
eat

# FOLLOWING JESUS' EXAMPLE

## LEARN IT

**START** with this dove and draw a trail that tells what happened when Jesus was baptized.

"AND THERE CAME

A VOICE

FROM

HEAVEN:

## PRAY IT

**IF YOU ARE NERVOUS** about being baptized, talk with a parent and then pray together, asking the Lord to give you courage!

BELOVED SON.

IS MY

THIS

I TAKE

DELIGHT

IN HIM!"

MATTHEW 3:17

Find and read Matthew 3:13-17 in your Bible. Who is being baptized? JESUS! He was baptized to show people what they should do after they become Christians. What did God do when Jesus was baptized? Read Matthew 3:17.

# FOLLOWING JESUS' EXAMPLE

**LEARN IT**

**DRAW A LINE** from the word to the picture. Did you know that people can get baptized in any of these places?

LAKE

SWIMMING POOL

CHURCH BAPTISTRY

RIVER

**BONUS:**
Did you know missionaries sometimes have to baptize new Christians in a ...

**LIVE IT**

**ASK A PARENT** or senior adult to tell you about his baptism. Ask where he was baptized and who baptized him.

# FOLLOWING JESUS' EXAMPLE

**DO IT**

**MANY IMPORTANT** words about the Lords Supper are in I Corinthians 11:23-26. Read the verses with a parent and search for words from the Word Bank in the puzzle.

```
B R E A D Y X M T V S T T A S
C W L Q F E P G H I H H T E Q
P P V M Y V K J X A M B T T H
X O M S Z S G A N R Y Q U O D
R S Y Z P G R K J L V N P O T
H T D H S B S L O R D P O S F
G J O H E G C W W O A L A L T
U B B M B O D Y W Y B N Q W O
D R R F T H A N K S U S N P J
V O A X D A E R B Y K Z W D E
P K O J E S U S M L Q J T W S
P E F Q B R O K E T U I R Q U
M N T T B I C S T Z I S Y P S
D A E V B J W D R O L M U D B
B L O O D V O S L J F C U P G
```

## WORD BANK

BLOOD
BODY
BREAD
BROKE
CUP
JESUS
LORD
THANKS

**LEARN IT**

1 JOHN 2:6

**DO YOU REMEMBER** our memory verse from this week? Write down as much of it as you can remember. Check your work by looking at 1 John 2:6.

# FOLLOWING JESUS' EXAMPLE

## LEARN IT

During baptism and the Lord's Supper, you should show respect for God and for what He has done for you. Play the following game with a family member or a friend. Flip a coin onto the grid and tell if the picture shows something that is respectful (give a thumbs-up) or disrespectful (give a thumbs-down) to do during baptism or the Lord's Supper.

The way in which you take part in the Lord's Supper is important. Here are some things you can do: Remember why Jesus chose to die and how much He loves you. Confess your sins and ask God to forgive you. Thank God for Jesus. Be quiet so you and the people around you can think about Jesus and pray to God. Listen to your pastor's words. By listening you will begin to understand more about the meaning of the Lord's Supper.

**FIND IT**

Grab your Bible and find 1 Corinthians 10:31.
Tell a parent or friend how you plan to act during the next Lord's Supper at your church.

**PRAY IT**

Ask God to help you show respect and honor to Him during baptism and the Lord's Supper.

# WEEK 4

## I'M A PART OF A CHURCH

A church does the work of God together. Churches meet to learn more about God, Jesus, and the Bible. A church plans to tell other people about Jesus. Churches have different ways of doing the work of God. Churches meet in many different kinds of buildings, but a church is not a building.

The Book of Acts tells the story of the very first Christian church. A group of believers were together, and God sent the Holy Spirit to them. The Holy Spirit helped Peter to stand up and tell a big crowd of people about Jesus, and many people believed and repented. Then, the new believers were baptized and joined with the other believers to make the first church. The first church and the church today are made up of people who have trusted Jesus as Savior and have been baptized.

**LEARN IT** CHURCH – a group of baptized believers

**KNOW IT** Look up Acts 2:42 in your Bible and memorize it this week. This verse tells four things that the early church did together. Write the four things in the blanks below:

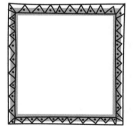   

Think about the things you like to do and the things you are good at doing. Now think how you can use your abilities to help your church do what God wants it to do.

### ABOUT MY CHURCH!

Read the questions and fill in your answers in the spaces provided.

What is the name of your church? _____

Why do you like your church? _____

How long has your family been a part of your church? _____

Who is the pastor of your church? _____

Who are your Sunday School teachers? _____

What are the names of some of your friends at church? _____

Everyone in the church works together to help others hear about Jesus. What can you do to help your church? Check the boxes of things you think you can do to serve your church.

☐ Keep the church building clean.

☐ Help welcome visitors when they arrive.

☐ Say hello to new kids at Sunday School and invite them to sit with you.

☐ Give an offering.

☐ Ask to help your Sunday School teacher before or after class.

☐ Say thank you to your pastor.

☐ Visit church members who are sick.

**PRAY IT** Thank God for a church that helps you learn more about God, Jesus, and the Bible. Ask God to help you know what He wants you to do to help others in your church.

_____

_____

_____

_____

**FIND IT**

**CAN YOU** remember our memory verse? Hint:  Acts 2:42 Match the following four things that the early church did together with the picture below.

| FELLOWSHIP | BREAKING OF BREAD | APOSTLES TEACHING | PRAYER |
|---|---|---|---|
|  |  |  |  |

**DO IT**

**PLACE A CHECK** in each box by the activities you participate in at your church.

- ☐ Sunday School
- ☐ Kids' Worship
- ☐ Worship Service
- ☐ Camp
- ☐ Missions class
- ☐ Children's choir
- ☐ Service Projects
- ☐ Mission Trips
- ☐ Other _____

**PRAY IT**

**PRAY,** thanking God for the people at the church you attend.

Thank Him for your pastor and your teachers at church. Thank God for a church that helps you learn more about God, Jesus, and the Bible.

**CHURCH** — a group of baptized believers. A church does the work of God together. Churches meet to learn more about God, Jesus, and the Bible. A church plans to tell other people about Jesus. Churches do God's work in different ways. Churches meet in many different kinds of buildings, but a church is not a building.

## CODE KEY:

| | |
|---|---|
| A | ◉ |
| B | ☽ |
| C | ◎ |
| D | ♣ |
| E | ♥ |
| F | ★ |
| G | ✚ |
| H | ✸ |
| I | 🎆 |
| J | 🍃 |
| K | ⊙ |
| L | ☺ |
| M | ◎ |
| N | ⚡ |
| O | ⁞⁞⁞ |
| P | ☆ |
| Q | ☀ |
| R | → |
| S | ← |
| T | ≣ |
| U | ∿ |
| V | ◎ |
| W | ☆ |
| X | ◉ |
| Y | 🎇 |
| Z | ✿ |

WEEK 4 * DAY 2

# I'M PART OF A CHURCH

## LEARN IT

**JESUS GAVE** specific instructions for His followers. Match each shape to a letter to find out what every baptized believer in the church should do.

**EPHESIANS 6:20** ☆ → ◎ ✸

**ACTS 22:15** ≣ ♥ ☺ ☺

**MATTHEW 28:19** ✚ ⁞⁞⁞

**1 JOHN 4:7** ☺ ⁞⁞⁞ ◎ ♥

**PHILIPPIANS 4:4** → ♥ 🍃 ⁞⁞⁞ 🎆 ◎ ♥

The Book of Acts in the New Testament tells four things the first churches did. Find those four things in Acts 2:42. List them here. They devoted themselves to the . . .

_____  _____  _____

What are three things that you can do to help at your church right now? If you need ideas, talk to your parents or another adult from your church. They can help you think of ways to help. Print three things that you can do to help your church.

_____  _____  _____

## LEARN IT

**ANSWER** each question to find people who work together to help your church run smoothly.

**WHO CLEANS YOUR CHURCH BUILDING?**

**WRITE THE NAME OF A SUNDAY SCHOOL TEACHER.**
(other than your own teacher)

**WHO PRINTS THE CHURCH BULLETINS?**

**WHO PLAYS THE PIANO?**

**WHO IS PREPARING TO GO ON A MISSION TRIP?**

**WHO WELCOMES GUESTS AT THE FRONT DOOR?**

**WRITE THE NAME OF A DEACON.**

2 Corinthians 6:1 tells us that we work together with Jesus. Being a part of a church means that we work together to tell others about Jesus!

# I'M PART OF A CHURCH

## LEARN IT

**INTERVIEW** someone in your family or neighborhood who is a member of your church.

Name of person interviewed:

How long have you been a member of this church?

When did you trust Jesus to be your Savior?

When were you baptized? Where were you baptized?

Have you ever served at church? What did you do?

What does being a church member mean to you?

Do you think you are too young to make a difference? Just because you are young doesn't mean that you cannot do things at church and in your community. You are an important part of your church! Think about the things you like to do and the things you are good at doing. Now think how you can use your abilities to help your church do what God wants it to do.

## PRAY IT

**THANK GOD** for your church family and pray especially for the person you interviewed.

**LIVE IT**

**COMPLETE THE MAP** below by drawing a place you go in your community in each of the blank spots. Write the name of the place below your drawing.

MUSEUM

HOSPITAL

HOME

LIBRARY

**DO IT**

Ask a parent to help you make cookies and deliver them to a church member.

**USING** a different colored marker, write beside each location the name of a person you could tell about Jesus and how you can serve him.

# WEEK 5

## LIVING AS A CHRISTIAN

What would happen if you only ate cookies and ice cream and never brushed your teeth or exercised? Would you be healthy? No! Eating fruits and vegetables, brushing your teeth, and staying active can help you keep your body healthy. But did you know that Christians have to keep their spiritual bodies healthy too? Bible study, prayer, worship, and giving are four things that Christians do to keep a healthy relationship with God.

**LEARN IT**

THE BIBLE is God's message about Himself.

BIBLE STUDY is reading the Bible to learn what God says.

PRAYER is talking and listening to God.

WORSHIP is how you show God how much you love Him.

GIVING is sharing your money, time, talents, and possessions with others.

**KNOW IT**  Find John 14:15 in your Bible. Commit to know this verse by memory by the end of the week. What does Jesus say you should do if you love Him? Write your answer in the blank: _____

BIBLE STUDY: The Bible helps you know more about God and Jesus and what they are like. The Bible also tells you what God wants you to do. The Bible is a book different from any book ever written. God told the men who wrote the Bible what to write. He helped them know how to say the things He wanted them to say. Every story in the Bible is true and tells about men and women who learned to follow God. The people you read about in the Bible lived a long time ago. You can learn from their lives.

**DO IT**  There are many ways to study your Bible. Sometimes, you will find words in the Bible that you do not understand. You can ask a parent or another adult for help to read your Bible. Look at the chart on page 62 and write one way from each section on how you can study your Bible.

**1**

Study one Bible book.

_____

_____

**2**

Study one Bible verse.

_____

_____

**3**

Study one person from the Bible. _____

_____

**PRAYER:** As a Christian, you can use your words to talk to God. One way to pray is to ask God for things. What are some things you have asked God for? Write two or three of them here.

_____

_____

God not only wants you to ask Him for things, He wants you to listen to Him. God speaks to you as you read and learn verses from your Bible. God also speaks through other people. When you are quiet and listen to Him, you will understand what He is telling you.

**WORSHIP AND GIVING:** How do you let others know you love them? Do you treat them in a nice way? Do you do things for them? Do you say, "I love you"? How do you let God know you love Him? You can show God you love Him in many ways. Showing your love to God is called worship.

When you think about worship and giving, you might just think of when you sing in church, or when you put your money in the offering plate. Those are two great ways that Christians worship and give, but they are not the only ways! You can worship by using the special talents God has given you! There are also many things you can give. You can give not only by sharing your money, but also by sharing your talents and time with others.

**DO IT**

In the space below, list some ways you want to worship and give.

_____

_____

_____

**PRAY IT**

Thank God for the Bible. Ask Him to help you understand the words you read from it each day. Thank God for always hearing you when you pray. Ask Him to help you use your talents and gifts to worship Him and share with others.

_____

_____

_____

_____

# LIVING AS A CHRISTIAN

## LEARN IT

### FILL IN THE BLANKS

using the following words: worship, give, study the Bible, and pray.

To grow as a healthy disciple I can:

## FIND IT

**WITH AN** adult's help, find John 14:15 in the Bible and answer the following questions.

 What do you do if you love God?

 Do you know any of His commands?

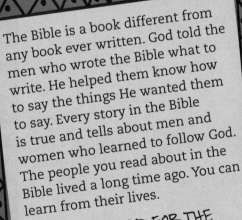

The Bible is a book different from any book ever written. God told the men who wrote the Bible what to write. He helped them know how to say the things He wanted them to say. Every story in the Bible is true and tells about men and women who learned to follow God. The people you read about in the Bible lived a long time ago. You can learn from their lives.

THANK GOD FOR THE BIBLE. ASK HIM TO HELP YOU UNDERSTAND THE WORDS YOU READ FROM IT EACH DAY.

How do you learn about Jesus? You can go to Sunday School, other groups for children at church, and worship services. You can pray and read your Bible. The Bible helps you know more about God and Jesus and what they are like. The Bible also tells you what God wants you to do.

# LIVING AS A CHRISTIAN

### ꙮ DO IT

**FIND** the healthy habits of a disciple.

```
A S T U D Y S K Y G O
P V E M C B E B T U O
R T L Q W O R S H I P
A A L I S T V J N S D
Y L Z G I V E E L K F
```

**WORD BANK:**

Pray
Serve
Worship
Study
Give
Go
Tell

**LEARN IT**

**WHAT IS WORSHIP?** Worship means you show God how important He is and how much you love Him. Circle the ways you can worship God.

PRAY

TELL A FRIEND ABOUT JESUS

READ MY BIBLE

SERVE

GIVE TO OTHERS

SING

I CAN WORSHIP GOD MANY WAYS!

# LIVING AS A CHRISTIAN

## PRAY IT

Dear God, help me to live by following your commands and showing Your love to others.

**LIVE IT**

With an adult's help, think of someone who needs to know Jesus' love.

Write his/her name here: _____

Now, what can you do to show love to that person? Circle an idea below and ask your parent to help you do it.

Look at the pictures below. Circle the pictures of places that you can pray.

CHURCH  PARK  GAME  FAIR  HOSPITAL  SCHOOL

Now open your Bible to 1 Thessalonians 5:17. When does it say to pray? Look back at the pictures you circled. Did you circle all of them? No matter what time of the day it is, where you are, or who is around you, you can pray.

Bake Cookies

Rake leaves

Help him wash his car

Walk her dog

Read a book to her

Tell him about Jesus

# LIVING AS A CHRISTIAN

### LEARN IT

**FILL IN** the missing letters! Match the color of each letter to the color of the blanks to find an important fact about living as a Christian.

**KEY CODE**  A E I O U

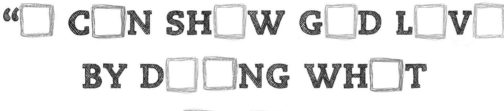

"□ C□N SH□W G□D L□V□ BY D□□NG WH□T H□ S□YS."

**PRAY IT** **DEAR GOD,** help me to do what You say.

**LEARN IT** **WHERE** can you learn what God says? Check the places you learn what God's Word says.

# LIVING AS A CHRISTIAN

## FIND IT

**READ** Philippians 4:13 and fill in the blanks to discover how to do what God says!

" _____ AM ABLE TO DO _____ THINGS THROUGH _____ WHO _____ ME." PHILIPPIANS 4:13

## LIVE IT

**WRITE** the names of five friends you can pray for.

Now, pray for them to know Jesus and show His love to others! What other ways, besides praying, can you live as a Christian? Write your answer below each picture.

_____ : _____ : PRAYING : _____

# WEEK 6

## SHARING YOUR TESTIMONY

What is the greatest news you have ever heard? Did you want to keep the news to yourself? No, you wanted to tell everyone! It is hard to keep good news to yourself.

Locate Luke 8:39 in your Bible. What does the verse say? Jesus told a man to tell everyone what God had done in his life. Telling everyone what God has done in your life is your testimony. Because you are a Christian, you can tell other people about your experience. Your story of how you became a Christian is important to tell. No one else has a story like yours!

Answering these questions can help you write your testimony. If it is too many words for you to write by yourself, ask a parent or another adult to write the words exactly as you say them. You might choose to video or audio record your answers.

**LEARN IT**    TESTIMONY [Tess tuh mow nee] telling about what God has done in your life
HOLY SPIRIT is the Spirit of God who helps people understand and receive God's plan of salvation.

**KNOW IT**    Find Mark 16:15 in your Bible and read it aloud. What does Jesus tell Christians to do? As you memorize Mark 16:15 this week, try to share it with a friend who needs to hear about Jesus.

**DO IT**   Write your answers to the following questions, or talk about them with a parent. Answering these questions will help you to share your testimony!

When did you first start thinking about becoming a Christian?

Why did you think that you needed to become a Christian?

Explain what happened when you became a Christian.

How is your life different since you became a Christian?

How would you help someone know how to become a Christian?

**PRAY IT**   Thank God for sending Jesus to save you. Ask God to help you tell others about Jesus and about how He makes a difference in your life.

# SHARING YOUR TESTIMONY

### LEARN IT

**LOOK** in the word bank. Find the item that goes with the picture under each line.

## WHAT IS A TESTIMONY?

_____ _____ STORY _____

_____ _____ _____

_____ _____ _____

### PRAY IT

## THANKING GOD FOR YOUR STORY

**THANK GOD** for showing you His love.

**THANK GOD** for letting you know about Jesus.

**THANK GOD** for giving you His Word, the Bible.

**THANK GOD** for forgiving your sins.

## WORD BANK

Find the picture on the left that is the best match for each picture below, and write the word in the blank.

STORY · HOW · CHANGED · LIFE · OF · TELLING · THE · HAS · YOUR · JESUS

# SHARING YOUR TESTIMONY

**DO IT**

Everyone's life story is different. Some people hear about Jesus from their parents. Some hear about Jesus from a friend, a missionary, or even a movie. Some people will never hear about Jesus unless you tell them.

**PICK ONE** of the children below. Follow the path that child is on. Notice how many people share their God Story with the child. To whom will you tell your God Story?

**LEARN IT**

**PAWS—ITIVELY POWERFUL!** Read Mark 16:15, then put the words of this memory verse in order. The paw prints will help you.

 whole creation.'"  the  'Go into all  Mark 16:15  gospel  "Then He [Jesus] said   to  world and preach  them [His Disciples]

# SHARING YOUR TESTIMONY

## FIND IT

### READ Acts 4:1–20.
### I CANNOT STOP!

Jesus visited the disciples after He rose from the grave. He told the disciples to tell people about God's love. He wanted them to teach more people about God's ways. Right away, they began to do the work Jesus asked them to do. They preached to big crowds in the cities. They answered new friends' questions about Jesus one-on-one. Wherever they went, they told their testimonies. Some people listened and believed. Some people did not like their message. Some people wanted to stop the disciples. In this story, important people in the city told Peter and John they could not talk about Jesus anymore. What was their answer? Follow the road signs to complete the verse.

△ FOR WE ARE _____

⯃ TO _____

SPEAKING ABOUT

⬨ WHAT WE HAVE _____

⬤ AND _____. ACTS 4:20

UNABLE

STOP

SEEN

HEARD

# SHARING YOUR TESTIMONY

## LEARN IT

**FOLLOW** the color code below to color in the squares in the grid.

When people are lost and can't find their way, what do they need most? Find John 14:6 and read why Jesus can help them.

| < | + | < | > | F | G | 3 | 5 | 9 | 9 |
|---|---|---|---|---|---|---|---|---|---|
| > | + | > | + | S | D | 7 | 6 | 4 | 2 |
| > | > | A | E | F | B | Q | T | 7 | 8 |
| < | > | X | J | D | M | A | L | 5 | 2 |
| + | < | + | + | W | E | 8 | 5 | 2 | 8 |
| > | + | < | > | Y | R | 0 | 6 | 9 | 3 |
| + | + | > | + | Q | T | 7 | 6 | 4 | 2 |

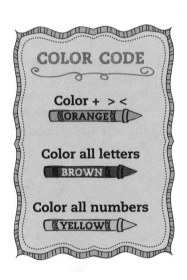

### COLOR CODE

Color + > <
**ORANGE**

Color all letters
**BROWN**

Color all numbers
**YELLOW**

**PRAY IT** **MAKE A LIST** of people you want to realize that they need Jesus' forgiveness. Ask God to change their darkness to light.

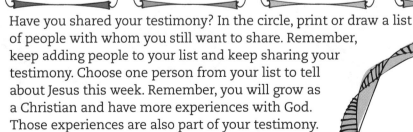

Have you shared your testimony? In the circle, print or draw a list of people with whom you still want to share. Remember, keep adding people to your list and keep sharing your testimony. Choose one person from your list to tell about Jesus this week. Remember, you will grow as a Christian and have more experiences with God. Those experiences are also part of your testimony. Continue to add to your story.

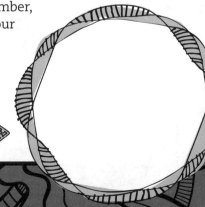

# SHARING YOUR TESTIMONY

## LIVE IT

In these pictures, kids are telling people about Jesus.

### CIRCLE
the way you'd most like to tell others about Jesus.

### PUT A STAR
over the person who reminds you most of someone from yesterday's Pray It list.

### PUT A CHECK
by one way you've never tried to share about Jesus.

MANY WAYS TO TELL, MANY PEOPLE TO REACH

## DO IT

### SHARE Your Testimony

Make your My God Story Box with your family. See page 63 for instructions. Find a friend who is willing to listen to you practice sharing your testimony. You can use your My God Story Box to help you tell your story.

## PRAY IT

### ASK GOD for Boldness

In Acts 4, the disciples prayed for boldness after the important people were mean to them. They did not give up sharing their testimonies. They did not want to be afraid. So they asked God to help them know what words to say. They asked God for courage. You can too. Take a moment to ask God to help you to tell your testimony.

# WEEK 7

## GOING ON MISSION

**Your child will learn about the importance of living on mission for God. Help frame the activity pages by explaining there are two kinds of missions your child can be involved in: 1) missions happening in your zip code and 2) missions happening in faraway places. Talk about ways your church is involved in both kinds of missions. If your church supports missionaries, spend time praying for them with your child.**

**Read Romans 10:14 together. Discuss that while mission activities may look different from one location to the next, all mission work is to help people hear and believe the good news of Jesus' gospel.**

What does your church do to help others? What are some ways that your church can be a helper to people who live in the community? What about to people who live all around the world?

Sharing the gospel with people who have never heard about Jesus is one way that the church can help others. The people who do this important work are called missionaries. Some missionaries go on mission in other countries far away from their homes. Others travel to big cities in North America. You can be a Christian on mission in your community too!

Find 1 Corinthians 12:12-27. Ask your mom or dad or another adult to read these verses with you. The "body" that these verses are talking about is a way of describing the church. Think about your body. Every part of your body is important. When one part of your body is sick, you feel sick all over. When all the parts of your body are working right, you feel great and like you can do anything! So, how does that help describe the church? Each person in the church needs to do his or her part and work together, whether in your community or on mission around the world.

**LEARN IT**

A MISSIONARY is a person whom God calls in a special way to tell others about Jesus.

MISSIONS is going someplace to tell others that Jesus wants to rescue them from sin.

48

**KNOW IT** Find Matthew 28:19a in your Bible. This memory verse is a command from Jesus for Christians. Does Jesus want Christians to stay at home, or go out and help others? _____

_____

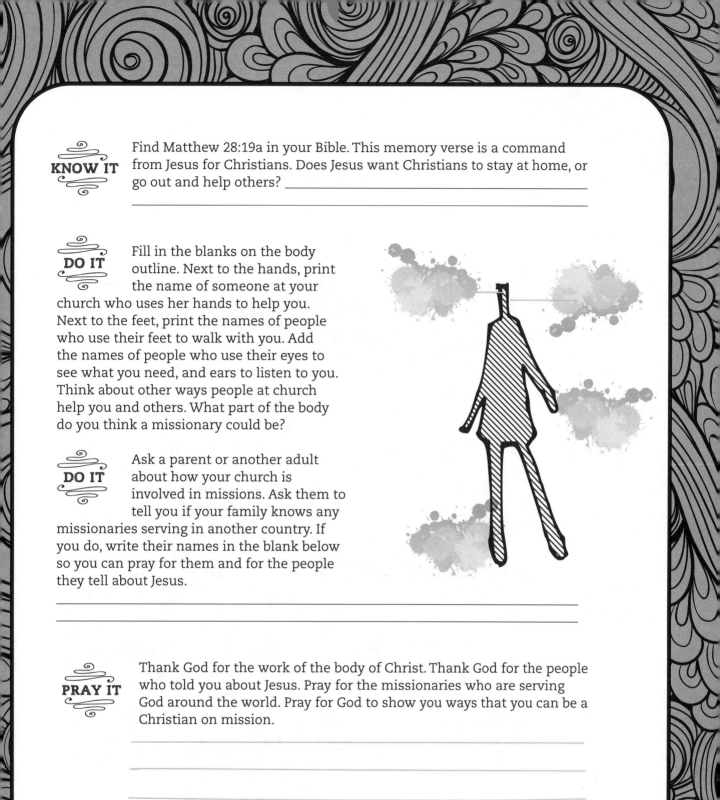

**DO IT** Fill in the blanks on the body outline. Next to the hands, print the name of someone at your church who uses her hands to help you. Next to the feet, print the names of people who use their feet to walk with you. Add the names of people who use their eyes to see what you need, and ears to listen to you. Think about other ways people at church help you and others. What part of the body do you think a missionary could be?

**DO IT** Ask a parent or another adult about how your church is involved in missions. Ask them to tell you if your family knows any missionaries serving in another country. If you do, write their names in the blank below so you can pray for them and for the people they tell about Jesus.

_____

_____

**PRAY IT** Thank God for the work of the body of Christ. Thank God for the people who told you about Jesus. Pray for the missionaries who are serving God around the world. Pray for God to show you ways that you can be a Christian on mission.

_____

_____

_____

_____

# GOING ON MISSION

**LIVE IT**

**FOLLOW** the path to discover what the on-mission people are doing to show and tell about God's love. In the final box, draw yourself doing an on-mission project, like praying for your adopted country or making a care package.

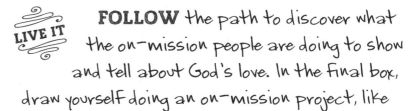

Helping a little sister or brother | Sharing about Jesus in other countries | _____ | Serving food to hungry families | Telling a friend about Jesus | Praying for a hospital patient

# GOING ON MISSION

## LEARN IT

All around the world, people need to hear about Jesus. They have other needs too. Draw a line matching the things listed below to the area of the world that needs those things. (Many of the items listed are needed by more than one area of the world. We just included one location for each need.) Can you tell the continent or country of each need?

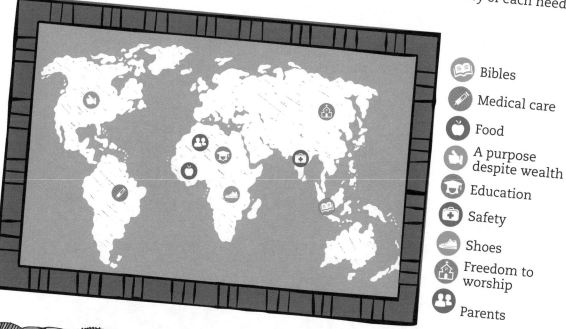

📖 Bibles

💉 Medical care

🍎 Food

👍 A purpose despite wealth

🎓 Education

🧰 Safety

👟 Shoes

⛪ Freedom to worship

👥 Parents

## DO IT

### YOU CAN DO IT!

This girl is thinking of some things she can do well. Can you find them? Circle the things she is thinking about. Then circle the things you can do well. God can use these talents to help you tell people about His love and forgiveness.

# GOING ON MISSION

## LIVE IT

Many groups work to help people who have needs. Not all groups that help people tell about Jesus. When you work with or give to missions, check for one important goal. What is that?

**DISCOVER** the answer by matching the flags on the left to the flags on the boats.

# GOING ON MISSION

**LIVE IT**

## WRITE THE NAMES

of the items below. Then circle the word "go" in each word.

Write places you would like to go to tell people about Jesus.

**PRAY IT**

## CIRCLE PLACES

in North America where you know missionaries. Draw a heart over the place you chose to pray for this week. Circle in the place where you live. Pray for missionaries in North America and around the world.

# GOING ON MISSION

## DO IT

**PICK** one of the goals below. Do what you can to support missions.

**WHAT CAN I DO?**

Offer to do extra chores, sell lemonade, bake cookies, or wash your neighbors' cars to earn money for a missions offering.

With the help of an adult, take small flower arrangements to people in an elder care facility. When you hand them out, say that you wanted them to feel God's love. Ask if you can pray for them.

Pray for missionaries around the world and for people in your adopted country to hear about Jesus.

Make a care package with a stuffed animal, a box of bandages, and a note about God's love. Give the care package to a local shelter or emergency room to give to a child in need.

**FIND IT**

**FIND** Romans 10:14. Read the verse aloud.

What does the world need most? Find the answer by finding your way through the maze.

The world needs ...

more
workers
to tell
people
that I am happy.
to build
money
to spend
on
about
Jesus.
give offering
a big
church.

# WEEK
# 8

# TRAVELING ON

How many people in the world are perfect?

If you said zero, you are right!

Even kids who never get in trouble at school or adults who make rules for you to follow are not perfect. Jesus is the only perfect person who ever lived. He came to earth to take the punishment for all the sin of the imperfect people. That means that even though you are a Christian now, Jesus knows you won't be perfect. You will still mess up, but now you trust in a perfect Savior who will forgive your sins.

Imagine that you had an important homework assignment, and you forgot to do it. Your consequence may be that you receive a bad grade or that you stay in from recess. But if your teacher chose not to enforce consequences, even though you deserved it, she showed you mercy.

What if instead of receiving a bad grade, she gave you an A+? You wouldn't deserve that at all! She would be giving you not only mercy, but grace. In the same way, Jesus gives Christians grace and mercy when they sin. Jesus provided mercy by taking the punishment for our sins, and He gives grace by offering a free gift of forgiveness.

**LEARN IT**
GRACE is receiving a blessing that you don't deserve.
MERCY is not receiving the punishment that you do deserve.

**KNOW IT** — Find Ephesians 5:1 in your Bible. An "imitator" is a person who copies someone else. What can you do to be an imitator of God this week?

**DO IT** — Match the word with its definition to review what you have learned over the past eight weeks!

1. CHRISTIAN

2. SAVIOR

3. SIN

4. LORD'S SUPPER

5. BAPTISM

6. REPENT

7. TESTIMONY

8. PRAYER

9. MERCY

10. GRACE

A. to turn from disobeying God to obeying Him ____

B. actions, attitudes, words, or thoughts that do not please God ____

C. talking to God and listening to Him ____

D. telling about your experience ____

E. a special time to help Christians remember Jesus' death ____

F. the name given to a person who has asked Jesus to be his Lord and Savior

G. Jesus, the person who paid the penalty for your sin ____

H. receiving a blessing that you don't deserve

I. not receiving the punishment that you do deserve

J. obeying God by being put under water to show that you have become a Christian

**PRAY IT** — Thank God for the grace and mercy He gives you when you sin. Ask Him to help you as you continue your journey as a new Christian.

_____

_____

_____

_____

# TRAVELING ON

**DO IT**

## DRAW A LINE

along the path to find all the places God is with you.

FRIEND

SCHOOL

YMCA

HOME

CHURCH

PARK

---

**PRAY IT**

Dear God, Help me to always turn to You when I have questions. Thank You for always being with me!

---

**LEARN IT**

## FILL IN THE BLANKS

to complete the memory verse. Then write your memory verse on an index card and say it to an adult each day this week.

"Therefore, be [          ] of [    ], as dearly loved [          ]."

Ephesians 5:1

# TRAVELING ON

## FIND IT

FIND and read each verse to help you fill in each circle with the answer from the Word Bank. Think about the definitions of grace and mercy.

What is grace? **GETTING GOOD THINGS YOU DON'T DESERVE**

Acts 20:32 says that the message of grace can

**WORD BANK FOR VERSES**

gives

Jesus

show

blesses

forever

for generations

build you up

John 1:17 says that God gives grace through

Psalm 84:11 says that the Lord _____ grace.

What is mercy? **NOT GETTING PUNISHMENT YOU DESERVE**

Matthew 5:7 says that God _____ the merciful.

Isaiah 30:18 says that the Lord will _____ mercy.

Luke 1:50 says God's mercy lasts _____

## PRAY IT

**DEAR GOD,** Help me to learn about the grace and mercy You've given me. Please help me to show grace and mercy to others.

# TRAVELING ON

## LEARN IT

**LOOK AT** the images below. Place a check mark next to the things that will help you in your journey as a Christian.

READING GOD'S WORD

GOING TO CHURCH

PRAYING

BEING AROUND OTHER CHRISTIANS

ASKING QUESTIONS

## DO IT

**FIND** the following terms in the word search below.

### WHAT IS THE WORD?

**WORD BANK**

Confess
Forgive
Mercy
Grace
Journey

| | | | | | | |
|---|---|---|---|---|---|---|
| S | B | Y | Y | T | Y | L |
| C | O | N | F | E | S | S |
| Y | G | Z | Z | T | R | M |
| F | O | R | G | I | V | E |
| T | V | U | A | B | Y | R |
| L | B | K | V | C | O | C |
| J | O | U | R | N | E | Y |

# TRAVELING ON

## LIVE IT

**THINK ABOUT QUESTIONS** you may have about life as a Christian. Make a list. Then sit down with an adult and ask him to help you answer the questions. Before you start, pray together that God would help you understand.

## FIND IT

**LOOK UP** Jeremiah 29:11-13.
Fill in the blanks to learn more about God's plans.
(HINT: you, plans, future, all, hope, listen, Me, knows, heart)

GOD HAS [ ] FOR YOU. HE ALREADY [ ] THEM.

GOD WANTS TO GIVE YOU A [ ] AND A [ ].

[ ]

WHEN YOU PRAY TO GOD, HE PROMISES TO [ ] TO YOU.

WHEN YOU SEEK GOD, HE SAYS, " [ ] WILL FIND [ ] "

YOU SHOULD SEARCH FOR GOD WITH [ ] OF YOUR [ ]

HOW DO YOU FEEL KNOWING GOD HEARS YOU?

## LIVE IT

**CHOOSE** from the following words to help you find your answer: serve, tell, love, help.

### WHAT IS THE GOAL
### OF LIFE AS A CHRISTIAN?

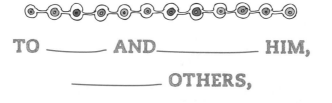

TO _____ AND _____ HIM,

_____ OTHERS,

AND _____ THEM TO DO THE SAME.

Because I am a Christian doesn't mean I will never sin again. It means I am forgiven for my sins as soon as I ask God. God still loves me, even when I mess up. He is never far away. He gives me strength to live for Him.

How do I receive forgiveness from God?_____

All people can receive forgiveness from God if they ask. When you pray and ask God to forgive you, don't forget your friends who need to know Him— pray for them too!

Who do you know who needs to know Jesus?

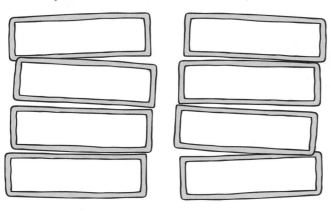

# HOW Do I Study MY BIBLE?

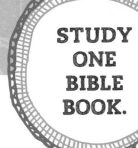 STUDY ONE BIBLE BOOK.

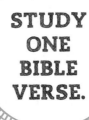 STUDY ONE BIBLE VERSE.

 STUDY ONE PERSON.

**WHO**
wrote the book and when was the book written?

**WHAT**
is the book about?

**WHAT**
does the book say about God?

**WHAT**
people does the book tell about?

**HOW**
did the people act toward God?

**WHAT**
can you learn about God from the book?

**READ**
the verse from different Bible translations.

**WHAT**
are the important words in the verse?

**WHAT**
are the words you don't understand?

**WRITE**
the verse in your own words. What can you learn from the verse?

**WHEN**
and where did the person live?

**WHAT**
took place in the person's life?

**HOW**
did the person act?

**WHAT**
can you learn from the person?

# MAKING A MY GOD STORY BOX

You have a great memory, but sometimes having an object you can see will help you remember events better. If you don't create a box in class, you may want to make one at home. You can place items in the box that can help you remember the most important time in your life. As you look through this book, place items in your box that will help you remember what you learn.

## CREATING THE BOX

**YOU WILL NEED:**
- A plastic shoe box or an older child's or adult size shoe box≠
- Craft paper to cover the box if needed
- Clear tape
- Markers, crayons, stickers, or other items to use to decorate the box

**TO DO:**
- Use the supplies collected to decorate your box.
- Keep your box in a safe place and add items to it to help you remember when you trusted Jesus as your Savior and Lord and when you were baptized.
- Include your name on the box.

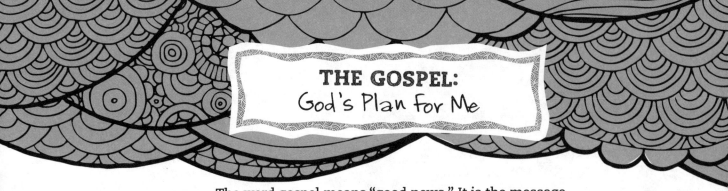

## THE GOSPEL:
### God's Plan For Me

The word gospel means "good news." It is the message
about Christ, the kingdom of God, and salvation.

**GOD RULES.** The Bible tells us God created everything, including you and me, and He is in charge of everything. Invite a volunteer to recite Genesis 1:1 from memory or read it from his Bible. Read Revelation 4:11 and Colossians 1:16-17.

**WE SINNED.** Since the time of Adam and Eve, everyone has chosen to disobey God. (Romans 3:23) The Bible calls this sin. Because God is holy, God cannot be around sin. Sin separates us from God and deserves God's punishment of death. (Romans 6:23)

**GOD PROVIDED.** Read John 3:16 aloud. God sent His Son, Jesus, the perfect solution to our sin problem, to rescue us from the punishment we deserve. It's something we, as sinners, could never earn on our own. Jesus alone saves us. Read Ephesians 2:8-9.

**JESUS GIVES.** Jesus lived a perfect life, died on the cross for our sins, and rose again. Because Jesus gave up His life for us, we can be welcomed into God's family for eternity. This is the best gift ever! Read Romans 5:8; 2 Corinthians 5:21; or 1 Peter 3:18.

**WE RESPOND.** We can respond to Jesus. "The ABCs of Becoming a Christian" is a simple tool that helps us remember how to respond when prompted by the Holy Spirit to the gift Jesus offers.

**ADMIT** to God that you are a sinner. The first people God created chose to sin and disobey God. Ever since then, all people have chosen to sin and disobey God. (See Romans 3:23.) Tell God you messed up and you are sorry for doing your own thing and turning away from Him through your thoughts, words, and actions. Repent, turn away from your sin. (Acts 3:19; 1 John 1:9) Repent doesn't just mean turning from doing bad things to doing good things. It means turning from sin and even from your own good works and turning to Jesus, trusting only in Him to save you.

**BELIEVE** that Jesus is God's Son and receive God's gift of forgiveness from sin. You must believe that only Jesus can save you and you cannot save yourself from your sin problem—not even by praying to God, going to church, or reading your Bible. Your faith or your trust is only in Jesus and what He did for you through His life, death, and resurrection. (See Acts 16:31; Acts 4:12; John 14:6; Ephesians 2:8-9.)

**CONFESS** your faith in Jesus Christ as Savior and Lord. Tell God and tell others what you believe. If Jesus is your Savior, you are trusting only in Him to save you. Jesus is also Lord, which means He is in charge and calling the shots in your life. You can start following Him and doing what He says in the Bible. You are born again into a new life and look forward to being with God forever. (Romans 10:9-10,13)